rupture and repair

rupture and repair

kaela prall

For my mother, and all the women who let me
stand on their shoulders.
And for everyone working hard to heal the
places that are hurting.

contents

do not be
afraid to
shatter;

there is freedom
in the falling.

-rupture and repair

rupture

there was no sudden moment
    of uncovering—the dusty attic
    relics stuffed in cardboard boxes
    the moment of truth.

i have always been here
    waiting
    invisible.
    i carried the stranger
    in the mirror until the door
    closed
    behind
    you.

    and i gasped

    because i didn't know i couldn't breathe

    i was never lost—
    it was only your hands around
    my neck.

    -breathing

i thought love was pain
because i'd been calling fear
by the wrong name.

-words matter

i am a raw thing
struggling to feel tame.
i am heat and sun
that wilts the delicate flower.
i pour water from my
eyes in apology.

- *grief*

you expressed your
suffering
in violence.

by the time you realized,
it was too late.

-abuse

you asked me once if i felt tricked
and i said nothing
because your hand was
over my mouth.

-*marriage*

it was your eyes that were most unfair,
finding me across a crowded room,
crinkling with secret jokes,
telling me everything you felt,
guiding me in like a ship on the sea.

it was your mouth, too, the way it bent
when you saw me laughing at you or
thinking of something
you said, ever walking the line
of loving me and loving someone else more.

it was your feet, eagerly showing
how fun it was to not walk alone,
to explore something new
with eyes that see you clearly
and a heart with a beat so near your own.

the unfair heart that pulled mine in
until it could not turn back, a star
whispering promises
to the adoring comet
then silent as it plummets into darkness

-you

when the promises
turn to
ash
in your mouth.

-time to go

this isn't
honesty

it's
   violence

-truth without love

what we don't know doesn't
kill us—
it takes us as a token,
a blind weeping fool.

we survive.
wiry creatures
rising from
still-glowing ash.
we make our own safety
in a world where we're not welcome.

you have things to do,
grieve on your way.
one of you was always
going to be lost.

fear is terrible for progress
but vital in war.

-fool

what if this is all there is?
what if this is all i am?
what if there is nothing left to say?

-the fear

did you think
i would believe
the leather lies
between your teeth?

-the end

wait

aching and stiff from waiting,
my muscles are crunching with it,
my ears are ringing
wait
wait
wait.

-here

you know you are free
yet here you are.

-living like a caged bird

i drank your
poison
      long enough
to forget
it was
      killing
me

-fugue

you ground me down to dust
then wondered why
i disappeared
when the
wind
came

-flight

i cannot explain myself
to you—

there are no words for
a walking wound
like me.

-silence

wrapped in the cool dark,
this binary balances on a whim,
two prayers.

they say equilibrium
only happens when stars align,
but we know it's been here all along.

i've guarded this chasma of secrets for as long as
there's been space,

eclipsed always
by the magnitude of light in you,
transfixed by the halo that follows.

i live in this penumbra
squinting in the afterglow.

you are the zenith,
pushing and pulling
your devoted satellite—
oblivious to the face
swallowed by the murk.

-aphelion

it's possible
        that
all I know now is
how to run away.

-learning

if he left a
void

wait

you are enough
to fill it

-the unbreaking

it's not that i
don't want to be here.

it's just that i don't
want to be here
like this.

-endless sky of gray

i wept rivers
into your desert,
and still
no flowers grew.

-*heartbreak*

the problem is this:
i don't know where
i end and
you begin.
are these your tears
or mine?

-disjunction

there is
no need
to
      smile
while you
burn

-tell the truth

i am haunted
by the years i wasted
doing what i
should.

-*poisoned expectations*

heavy with truth
and sorrow,
history humming in my chest.

-generations

if i plead with
myself
to listen to
the whispers
in my belly,
will i someday
be still enough
to hear?

-being

find peace here
or somewhere else:

i won't be your chaos

-enough

did you know?
you can
    collapse
from wanting—
holding pieces you
cannot feel,
giving in to greed.

-hunger

someday i'll find out
if there are poems
in joy, too.

-catharsis

repair

you know it's time when you no longer
recognize the face in the mirror:
too mild
too flat
too removed
from the no man's land inside.

when the tears won't come or won't stop,
when you're afraid of the answers,

find her then and you'll never lose her.

-your wild self

i will always be
separate
from you
because of you,
in spite of you.

-i belong to me

i can heal.
i will heal.
i am healing.

-*mantra*

when the feeling comes
back into my bones,
what a terror i will be.

-brace yourself

i didn't ask,
heart,
are you beating?
are you healing?
are you safe?

-checking in

this ink is
my healing.

-poem

i'm not sorry
for the
    things
i will say when
my tongue is
        loosed.

-truth

i weep
when the sun sets,
and still the moon comes.

-unconditional

the fist around
your heart
will go away.

-trauma

i went from
silence
      to "fuck you."
now i'm looking
for the
      in between.

-pendulum

remember when you
lived on his
obsession
and called it
love?

-then

i was all sharp
edges
to cut away
the
   shame

-rebirth

remember
when he
touches you
that you
are a wild thing and
do not need tamed

-please do not forget

do not brace

against

      the grief

pull it in

      close

and

  let it have

its way

-cry

love

this is a real
  living thing

hold it
        loosely
let it
        breathe

-yes, even this

you could be hurt

                  again

    it's part of the loving.

-worth it

my body
owes you
no apologies.

-sacred

when you're ready,
when your body knows you're safe,

then comes the remembering,
the nightmares,
the tearing,
the urge to break all over again.

if you find a place to unpack,
to hold your scarred hands out to the universe,
healing will come in the morning.

-medicine

that pain is
            courage
taking root.

-be brave

maybe the stars
are like us:
helplessly watching time
unfold,
wondering what magic
will happen next.

-signs

if your pulse
is too quick
for them,
your heart
too alive:

leave.

-you are not too much

break them
with the
    softest
        parts of you

-this is the revolution

you treated me like
twisted rope
      and dead
            ends

but he
touches me
        like
i am a universe in motion

-recognition

i am earth
　fire
　　sky
　　　rain
if it's magic you want
　　　　　　fuck off

-post-reformation

in the light of the morning,
i will memorize every line in your forehead
and watch your eyes as they dredge
my own for glimpses of familiar.

i will study the way your
lips move when you tell me your stories

and laugh
at all my jokes—
here in the soft rays of a weary sun.

you'll be studying me, too,
uncovering all the things i am tired of hiding
and holding them with a quiet
kindness that feels like love.

maybe we're the lucky ones
and we'll wake up in five years or ten and still
be in awe of the way
the morning light streams through.

-will it last

i cannot wait
to watch love turn
        your hair gray
and joy leave
        lines across your face

-grow old with me

tell me again
how i stole your air
and gave you life
all at once.

-beginning

you could destroy
me with a single look
and that's how i know.

-real

your fingers map
new trails,
whisper love
to a new universe.

-flesh and bone

i promise
every time i want to

                        run

i'll stay instead.

-i love you

you shrink
     expand
     you earn your stripes
     you ask for better
     build something
               out of nothing
     you hold possibility and
               mortality at once
     more powerful and beautiful
     in this tension
     wanting only
     to be filled
               with proof you are alive

-thank you

acknowledgements

each of these poems was written for you. thank you for reading them.

thanks to my mom, the gatekeeper—the one who has made a better life possible for all who come after.

thanks to my daughter—the one who taught me to love myself, to be gentle, to hold space for mistakes.

thanks to ryan, my person—the one who stands next to me, holds me up, sees me clearly.

thanks to becca—the one who sits with me in all the hard places.

thanks to michelle—the one who showed me how to show up for myself.

thanks to kelly—the one who believed in these pages first.

* * *

thanks to rupi and nayyirah—the ones who reminded me that poetry is the language my soul speaks.

thanks to deliliah—the one who made the flowers from my childhood fit perfectly in these pages.

thanks to eva—the one who edited it into order.

thanks to every mentor and therapist—the ones who walked with me through the trauma.

thanks to god—the source, the one who brings healing. i have found you here.

about the author

kaela is a writer, poet, and speaker based in wichita, ks. she has an MA in creative writing and currently works in strategic communications for non-profits and community organizations. her first book, *rupture and repair,* was released in march 2019. an avid storyteller, kaela's gentleness, vulnerability, and humor are evident in her writing. when she's not working on her upcoming novel, she plays guitar, travels, and visits bookstores. she lives in a cozy house with her boyfriend, her daughter, and their two dogs.

you can find her on instagram (@thewritekaela) or visit her website at kaelaprall.com.

Made in the USA
Columbia, SC
12 May 2019